YOU'D *never* BELIEVE IT BUT...

a rainbow is a circle

and other facts about colour

© Aladdin Books Ltd 1999

Designed and produced by
Aladdin Books Ltd
28 Percy Street
London W1P 0LD

CLD 21583
This edition was published in 2000 for
Colour Library Direct Ltd,
New Mill
New Mill Lane
Witney
Oxon
OX8 5TF

Designed by
David West • Children's Book Design
Designer Flick Killerby
Computer Illustrations
Stephen Sweet (Simon Girling & Associates)
Project Editor Sally Hewitt
Editor Liz White
Picture Research Carlotta Cooper
and Brooks Krikler Research

ISBN 0-7496-3403-0

Printed in Singapore

A CIP catalogue record for this book is
available at the British Library.

YOU'D *never* BELIEVE IT BUT...

a rainbow is a circle

and other facts about colour

Helen Taylor

Colour Library Direct

Contents

Introduction

Every day you see colours all around you, from dazzling plants and animals to colourful paints or lights. But have you ever thought about how to mix or split colours, or about the different messages colours can give you?

Join Jack and Jo as they learn about primary and secondary colours, rainbow colours and much, much more.

FUN PROJECTS Wherever you see this sign, it means that there is a project which you can do.

Each project will help you to understand more about the subject. You'd never believe it but... each project is fun to do, as well.

Colour everywhere

The world is a colourful place with blue skies, green leaves and brightly coloured flowers, birds and insects. Clothes, toys, cars and the things you use are often colourful too. Look all around you. How many different colours can you see? What is your favourite colour? Are there any colours you don't like?

My favourite colour is yellow.

The world would look very different without colour (above). Would it be duller or more interesting? Would it be difficult to live without colour?

You'd never believe it but...

There are perhaps as many as 10 million different colours; many surround you every day (left).

Guess what my favourite colour is.

SHADES OF COLOUR
Collect all kinds of colourful objects including paper and card. Sort them into groups of different colours. Are all the yellow objects exactly the same yellow? What about the blue objects? Every colour has many different shades. Make a collage using only yellow objects. Look at how many different shades of yellow there are!

Primary and secondary colours

Red, yellow and blue are very important colours. They are called the primary colours of paint. You can make lots of other colours by mixing these colours.

red + yellow
= orange

yellow
+ blue
= green

I want to make orange.

red + blue
= purple

When primary colours are mixed in pairs the colours they make are called secondary colours. Orange, green and purple are secondary colours.

You'd never believe it but...

Paints were used many thousands of years ago. Colours called pigments can be found in earth or rocks. Cave painters used these to paint the walls of caves.

Try mixing red and yellow.

MIXING PAINTS

It is surprising how many colours and shades you can make by mixing different amounts of primary colours together. Try to paint a picture using as many colours as you can make from just the primaries.

Mixing colours

You may not realise it, but often your brain will mix colours together for you! If you make a picture from lots of little different coloured dots, your brain mixes the dots together to form new colours. What colour do you think your brain will see if you mix red and blue dots?

I want to draw a green hat.

COLOUR WHEEL
Try making this colour wheel. Start with the primary colours. Then mix each pair of primary colours together to make the secondary colour in between. Opposite colours on the wheel can look brighter when placed next to each other.

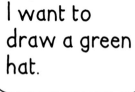

You'd never believe it but...

Look at a book, and you see solid colours, but under a magnifying glass you will see thousands of coloured dots.

Use yellow and blue dots.

The French artist Seurat used dots of colour to create images in his paintings. If you look at them close up, you only see the dots. But from a distance, the solid colour images appear.

Splitting colours

The coloured inks used in felt-tip pens are often a mixture of different colours. Usually they are made up of different amounts of primary colours. You can find out which colours were used in each pen.

> There's some blue in the green pen.

FINDING COLOURS

You will need kitchen towels, felt-tip pens and a glass of water. Draw a small dot with each pen onto a kitchen towel. Leave plenty of space between each dot. Drop a small amount of water onto the coloured dots. The water spreads out and carries the different colours different distances. How many different colours around each dot can you spot?

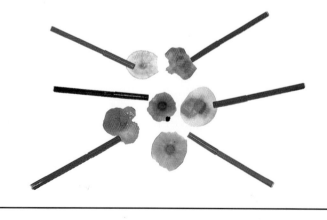

You'd never believe it but...

If ink is left at the scene of a crime, detectives can tell which pen it has come from by splitting the colours in the ink.

I'm turning the blobs into flowers.

Making colours

Dyes have a strong colour and are used to colour many things. The first dyes were made naturally by boiling plants like onions, grass and beetroot. Today we can buy dye in small packets of powdered chemicals. Dyes colour paint and the ink in felt-tip pens. Your clothes are coloured with dyes too.

> Did my jumper come from a yellow sheep?

Some rocks look colourful because they contain pigments. Paints and dyes contain pigments too, which can be used to change the colour of things.

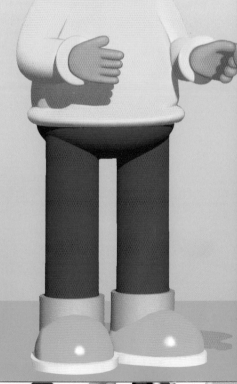

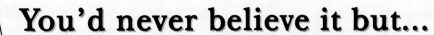

You'd never believe it but...

You can eat small beetles! A bright red dye called cochineal is made from grinding up small beetles. The cochineal beetle is tiny (left) and is used to make some food colouring, so you may have tasted it before!

No! The wool has been dyed yellow.

TIE DYE A HANDKERCHIEF

Ask an adult to chop up a beetroot and boil it so that the water becomes purple. Tie some string tightly around a handkerchief as shown. Dip it into the water and leave for a few minutes. Take it out and cut the string when it is cool. Dry it. Can you see how and where the dye has coloured the material a beetroot colour?

Rainbow colours

Mixing coloured lights produces new colours, too, but in a different way to mixing paints. We often say light is white, but really light is made up of all the seven colours of the rainbow: red, orange, yellow, green, blue, indigo and violet. We call these colours the spectrum.

When the Sun shines through raindrops, the water bends the white light and splits it into the different colours. A rainbow appears as a spectrum in the sky.

The Sun shining through the water makes a rainbow!

You'd never believe it but...

A rainbow is really a circle, not a bow. You can only see part of the rainbow from the ground. From an aeroplane a rainbow looks like a circle.

I can see seven different colours.

MAKING RAINBOWS

Blow bubbles in the sunshine. The light makes rainbows in the soapy skin of the bubbles.

Recognising colours

When light shines on an object, some of the rainbow colours are taken in, or absorbed, by it but other colours bounce back, or reflect, off it. We see the colours that bounce back off an object. This means you can only see colours if light shines on an object.

> I can't see the colour of my jumper in the dark!

Although we speak of seeing colours of objects, we do not actually see them. We see the light that bounces off them. For example, a red sock looks red because it reflects red light and absorbs the other colours. You only see the red light that reflects off the sock, so it looks red.

You'd never believe it but...

Animals like cats that hunt at night cannot see colour very well, but their eyes are very good at letting in light, which helps them to find their way in the dark.

You can see it's yellow if I shine my torch on it.

Inside your eyes, special cells called cones send messages to your brain about the colours you see. There are three types of cone. One type recognises red light, one blue and a third green.

Black and white

Some objects take in, or absorb, all the colours of the rainbow when light shines on them. If this happens, the object looks black. When all the colours of the rainbow bounce back, or reflect, off an object it looks white.

Sooty takes in all the colour from light, so he is black.

SPINNING TOP

Cut a circle out of card. Divide it into seven equal sections, colour each section a different rainbow colour. Push a short pencil through a hole in the centre. Spin the top. What happens? You see white because your brain mixes all the colours of the spectrum together.

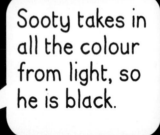

Light-coloured objects reflect a lot of light, but dark colours reflect little or no light. A photographic negative shows these areas in reverse, so black or dark objects look white and white or light objects look black.

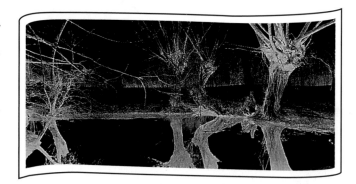

You'd never believe it but...

Over 300 years ago, Sir Isaac Newton proved white light is made from the colours of the rainbow. He split light through a glass prism and made a spectrum.

Snowy reflects all the colours, that's why he's white.

Coloured light

Glass (left), water and cellophane are all transparent materials. This means you can see through them. You can still see through transparent materials even if they are coloured, but the colour makes everything look different.

CHANGING COLOUR
Collect some coloured cellophane sweet wrappers. Flatten them out and look through them one at a time. The coloured cellophane becomes a filter. It only lets light of its own colour pass through it. If you look at an orange ball through a green filter, the ball looks dark. The green filter only lets green light through; the other colours are blocked so they look dark.

Ooh! Everything looks spooky!

You'd never believe it but...

Coloured filters can be put over a camera lens. Areas where there is a lot of light will show up the colour of the filter; other areas will appear darker.

Don't worry - it's only green and red lights!

Coloured filters are put over spotlights at the theatre to make exciting effects on the stage.

Colour in plants

Plants help to make the world look bright and colourful. But the colours in plants are not just there to look pretty, they have an important job to do. The stems and leaves of plants contain chlorophyll. It is a pigment that gives plants their green colour. Plants use chlorophyll and sunlight to make their own food.

Brightly coloured flowers send a message to birds and insects that there is food here! The birds and insects carry pollen from flower to flower. This means the flowers can make new seeds.

Watch out - a bee!

PLANT CHART

Make a chart of the colours in your garden or nearby park. How many different coloured plants are there? Which seem more popular with the birds, bees and butterflies? Why do you think this is?

colour	bird	bee	butterfly
	✓	✓✓	
		✓	
			✓✓
	✓		

You'd never believe it but...

Flowers of the yellow bee orchid are coloured to look like a female bee. This attracts the male bee to visit the flower and pollinate it.

Don't worry, it's visiting the colourful flowers.

Some plants use colours as a warning. The fly agaric toadstool is brightly coloured to warn animals that it is poisonous.

Colour in animals

When animals are coloured to match their surroundings we say they are camouflaged. It's difficult to spot a greeny brown frog in a pond because the colour of the pond matches its skin. Animals use camouflage to hide from their enemies or stalk their prey.

The Arctic Fox has a white coat in winter so it can hide in the snow. Its coat turns brown in summer so it is camouflaged against the soil.

STANDING OUT

The poison arrow frog is bright red. This warns its enemies to keep away. Pick out some clothes which you think make you look striking.

I almost didn't see you in those colours!

You'd never believe it but...

Chameleons can change the colour of their skin. They match their surroundings for camouflage and frighten enemies with the brightly coloured insides of their mouths.

That's because I'm camouflaged.

Male peacocks (above left) have bright feathers to attract a mate. Female peacocks have dull feathers to camouflage them from enemies when they are sitting on their eggs.

Colour messages

Colours can give us important information about what is happening all around us. The colour red usually warns us of danger. A red traffic light means stop and a green light means it's safe to go.

WAAAH!

MAKE A PAINT CHART

We say yellow is a warm colour, perhaps as it reminds us of the Sun. Cut out lots of colours. Place the colours you think are warm on one side of a piece of paper. Place the cold colours on the other side. Are there any colours you are not sure of?

How do you feel when you wake up and the sky is bright blue? Do you feel different when the sky is a dull grey? Colours can affect whether we feel happy or sad, cosy or uncomfortable.

Help - you look really scary!

You'd never believe it but...

Colours for advertisements can be used to make us feel happy, sad, excited or calm.

We sometimes use colours to describe how we feel. Have you ever felt 'sad and blue', or 'green with envy'? Can you think of any other expressions you use that use colours to describe your emotions?

Glossary

Absorb

To absorb means to take in. A sponge absorbs water. When light shines on an object, some of the colours in light are absorbed and we don't see them. If all the colours are absorbed, we see black.

Camouflage

Some animals use camouflage to hide from their enemies. The colours of their coats or feathers are the same as their surroundings, so they are very difficult to see. Animals also use camouflage to hide when they stalk their prey.

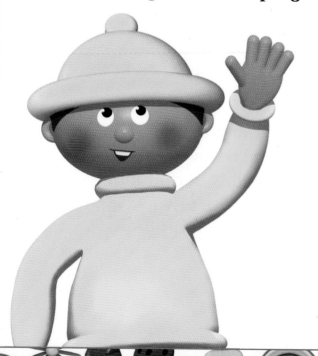

Cones

Cones are a special kind of cell in your eyes that are sensitive to light. You have three kinds of cone – one kind that detects red light, another that detects blue light and a third that detects green light.

Dye

We use dyes to colour paints, materials and many things we use. The colour to make dyes can come from natural things, such as rocks or plants, or it can be made using chemicals.

Filter

Filters are made from transparent or see-through materials, like glass or cellophane, that have been coloured. A filter only lets light of the same colour pass through it and it holds back the other colours. A green filter will only let through green light. A red filter will only let through red light.

Pigments

Pigments are natural colours found in soil, rocks, minerals and plants. They can be used to make dyes that colour the things we use.

Primary and secondary colours

The primary colours of paint are red, blue and yellow. The secondary colours of paint are the colours you make when you mix any two of the primary colours together. Red and yellow make orange. Blue and yellow make green. Red and blue make purple. Orange, green and purple are the secondary colours of paint.

Prism

A prism is a piece of glass with triangle-shaped sides. When white light shines through a prism, it bends and splits into the seven colours of the spectrum.

Rainbow

A rainbow is a spectrum in the sky. It is the arc we see in the sky when sunlight shines through raindrops. The raindrops bend the white light and split it into the seven colours of the rainbow.

Reflect

To reflect means to send back or bounce back. When light shines on an object, we see the colours in light that bounce back off that object. If all the colours in light bounce back, we see white.

Spectrum

White light can be split into the seven colours of the rainbow. We call these colours the spectrum.

Transparent

Some materials like glass or cellophane are transparent. This means that they let light through and we can see through them.

Index

PHOTO CREDITS

Abbreviations: t-top, m-middle, b-bottom, r-right,
l-left, c-centre
All the photography in this book is by Roger Vlitos
except the following pages: 9 -Frank Spooner Pictures; 11 - The
National Gallery; 15 & 28 - Pictor International; 17, 26, 27
both - Bruce Coleman Collection; 19b & 25 - Spectrum
Colour Library; 20-21 - Simon Roose; 23t -
Oxford Scientific Library.